"Careers in Information Technology: Database Administrator"

GoodMan, Volume 1

Patrick Mukosha

Published by Patrick Mukosha, 2023.

Title: "Careers in Information Technology: *Database Administrator*"

Is a Job as a Database Administrator worthwhile?

A career in information technology may be of interest to you if you want to work as a *Database Administrator*. A **Database Administrator** or DBA, is responsible for maintaining, securing, and operating databases and also ensures that data is correctly stored and retrieved.

In an organization, database administrators are crucial to the upkeep and storage of information. It's helpful to *become more knowledgeable* about the *duties of database administration* if you're considering a career in the field.

This can help you decide if it's a desirable employment prospect for you in a more educated manner.

Let's get more information in the book.

Copyright Notice

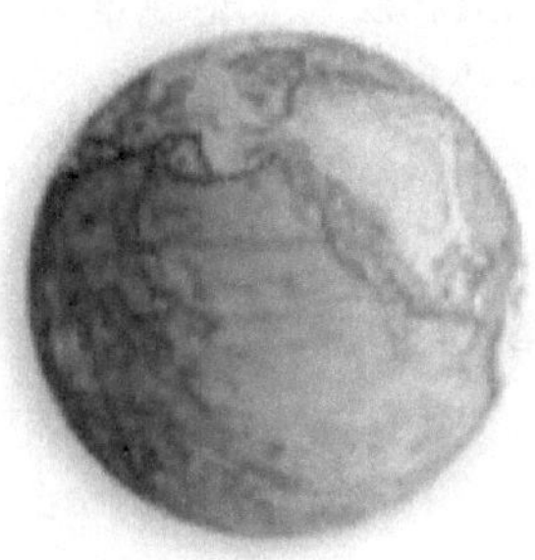

All Rights Reserved.

Trademarks

All terms mentioned in this book that are known to be trademarks or service marks have been appropriately capitalized. The Author and the publisher cannot attest to the accuracy of this information. Use of a term in this book should not be regarded as affecting the validity of any trademark or service mark.

Warning and Disclaimer

Every effort has been made to make this book as complete and as accurate as possible, but no warranty or fitness is implied. The information provided in this book is on as is basis. The Author and the Publisher shall have neither liability nor responsibility to any person or entity with respect to any loss or damage arising from the use the information contained in this book.

Author: Patrick Chisenga Mukosha PhD

Acknowledgements

The author is indebted to a large number of researchers, and consultants in the field of Information Technology (Database Administration) whose works were referred to in writing this book – and appears below and in the bibliography.

The author also would like to acknowledge the encouragement of my wife; Gracious Lumba Maboshe-Mukosha, my departed colleague and family friend; Bernard Chisanga (MHSRIP), and my children, whose comments and constructive criticism kept the author alive. The author also benefitted from the comments of several of my Network Engineering and ICT colleagues. They generously shared their insights and experiences in an evolving field where tacit knowledge is indispensable.

The author wishes to dedicate this book to his late younger sister, Loveness Mukosha (MHSRIP), for her dedication to transformational education. She died of Hypertension soon after completing her Bachelor's Degree in Education at the University of Zambia, in 2005. She's gone but not forgotten.

Special thanks go to Lionel Hugh Weston; my former Secondary School Teacher and Guardian, without whom I would never have had a strong education foundation in life. His contribution in my education career is immeasurable. I shall forever remain indebted to him and the entire Weston's family.

Abstract

In "Careers in Information Technology: *Database Administrator*," I provide an in-depth exploration of the exciting and continually evolving field of database administration within the Information and Communication Technology (ICT) industry. This one-page summary offers a glimpse into the key themes and insights presented in the book.

Unpacking the Role: The book commences by unravelling the role and significance of database administrators in today's technology-driven world. It highlights their vital role in the management, security, and optimization of data systems, underscoring the critical nature of their work in organizational success.

Essential Skills and Knowledge: To succeed in the database administration field, I discuss the fundamental skills and knowledge required. This includes proficiency in database management systems (DBMS), SQL, data modelling, as well as problem-solving and communication skills.

Adapting to Technological Advancements: In an era of rapid technological advancement, staying current is paramount. "Careers in Information Technology: *Database Administrator*" delves into the latest trends and innovations in database administration, such as NoSQL databases, cloud-based solutions, and big data technologies, ensuring that readers remain competitive in an ever-changing landscape.

Certifications and Career Progression: The book provides invaluable insights into certifications that can enhance career prospects, such as Oracle Certified Professional (OCP) and Microsoft Certified: Azure Data Engineer Associate. Additionally, it outlines potential career paths, including senior database administrator roles, data architect positions, or pivoting into roles like data analysis or business intelligence.

Challenges and Solutions: The challenges faced by database administrators are addressed comprehensively, from performance tuning and disaster recovery to data security and compliance.

Industry Dynamics and Networking: Understanding the dynamics of the ICT industry and building a professional network are essential for career growth. This book explores industry-specific knowledge and offers guidance on how to establish connections, navigate corporate culture, and pursue leadership roles.

Real-Life Experiences: Throughout the book, I share real-life case studies and anecdotes from seasoned database administrators. These stories offer readers a first-hand look into the practical aspects of the job, including complex problem-solving scenarios and innovative solutions.

"Careers in Information Technology: *Database Administrator*" is a valuable resource for individuals considering a career in database administration or seeking to advance their existing careers in this field. Whether you're a recent graduate, career changer, or a seasoned IT professional, this book equips you with the knowledge, skills, and strategies needed to excel in the ever-growing world of ICT. It serves as a guiding light, enabling you to make informed decisions, acquire the necessary skills, and thrive in the dynamic field of database administration.

Chapter 1: Introduction to Databases

The relational model (RM) of databases, first introduced by English computer scientist Edgar F. Codd in 1970, is a method for managing data that adheres to a structure and language consistent with first-order predicate logic. All data is represented as tuples that are organized into relations. A relational database is one that is set up using the relational model.

A table is created by grouping data into rows and columns in a relational database. Usually, data is organized into different tables that can be linked together using a primary key or a foreign key. These distinct identifiers show the many connections that exist across tables; these connections are typically shown through various kinds of data models. By combining various data points and summarizing business performance, analysts utilize SQL queries to help firms obtain new perspectives, streamline processes, and spot untapped opportunities.

Consider a scenario in which your business keeps a database table of customer data that includes account-level corporate information. Another table that lists every single transaction that corresponds to that account may also exist. When combined, these tables can reveal details about the various markets for a certain software product.

Customer ID, Company Name, Company Address, Industry, etc., might be the columns (or fields) for the customer table. Conversely, the columns for a transaction table could be Transaction Date, Customer ID, Transaction Amount, Payment Method, etc. The shared Customer ID field allows the tables to be connected. As a result, you may query the table to get useful information, including sales figures by industry or firm, which can guide message to potential customers.

Transactional databases, which execute orders or transactions collectively, are frequently linked to relational databases. A bank transfer is a frequent example that is used to demonstrate this. A specific amount is taken out of one account and deposited into another. Money is withdrawn and placed in whole, and no partial withdrawals or deposits are allowed during this transaction. Transactions have particular characteristics.

The following are examples of the acronym "ACID" properties:

- *Atomicity:* The treatment of all data changes as a single operation. That is, either every change is made or none of them are.
- *Consistency:* Data integrity is strengthened by consistency, which ensures that data is in the same condition from start to finish.
- *Isolation:* Because other transactions cannot see a transaction's intermediate state, concurrent transactions appear to be serialized.
- *Durability:* Changes to data that have been successfully completed after a transaction persist and cannot be undone, even in the event of a system failure.

These characteristics make transaction processing dependable.

a. What is a Relational Database?

Relational databases are a kind of database that let users access information kept in several tables linked together by a special ID, or "key." Users can assist with inventory management, shipping, and other tasks by using this key to unlock data entries associated with that key in another table. Users can enter SQL queries into relational database management systems (RDBMS) to obtain the data required for particular job functions.

Every table row in a relational database has a key. Data attributes are listed in the columns. Users can comprehend the relationships between data entries for tasks like product marketing, production, UX research, and more since each record includes a value for each attribute.

b. The Significance of Relational Databases

Relational databases play a crucial role in many facets of business, technology, and data administration. They are a fundamental part of contemporary information systems. The fundamental advantage of a relational database is its capacity to link data from many tables to provide insightful data. This strategy aids businesses of all sizes and sectors in identifying connections between multiple data sets from various departments to produce insightful information.

Data engineers create and construct systems for gathering, storing, and analysing data, including relational databases. They may assist all kinds of companies in gathering data by working in a variety of industries. This massive volume of data can then be handled by other job roles, including data scientists and analysts, who can use it to gain insightful knowledge.

Key elements of their relevance are as follows:

1. **Data Organization and Structure:** Relational databases offer a structured and organized method of managing and storing the data. Because data is saved in tables with predetermined schemas, consistency and integrity in data storage are maintained.
2. **Data Integrity**: By enforcing data integrity through restrictions and regulations, they make sure that the data entered into the database is correct, consistent, and meets predetermined criteria. By doing this, errors and data corruption are avoided.
3. **Querying and Retrieval**: Relational databases have strong querying capabilities, enabling users to quickly access, filter, and analyse data. Relational databases can be accessed using the standard language known as SQL (Structured Query Language).

4. **Scalability:** In order to accommodate growing data loads and user concurrency, relational databases can scale both vertically (by adding server resources) and horizontally (by splitting data across several servers).

5. **ACID Properties:** The ACID (Atomicity, Consistency, Isolation, Durability) properties they offer transactional support make sure that database operations are dependable and maintain data consistency.

6. **Data Relationships:** Relational databases are excellent at maintaining intricate relationships between data elements. They provide effective data retrieval and maintenance by allowing the formation of foreign keys and defining relationships between tables.

7. **Security:** Relational database management systems (RDBMS) are often developed with strong security measures, such as user authentication, authorization, and encryption, to secure sensitive data.

8. **Data Analysis and Reporting:** Relational databases are the cornerstone of data warehousing and business intelligence solutions, which in turn serve as the basis for data analysis and reporting. Using SQL queries, analysts can run complex data analyses and produce reports.

9. **Data Integration:** By offering a single platform for data storage and retrieval, they make it easier to integrate data from many sources. For applications that need to access several data sets, this is essential.

10. **Historical Data:** Relational databases are ideal for storing historical data because they enable businesses to monitor changes in their data over time.

11. **Compliance and Auditing:** Relational databases assist firms in meeting compliance requirements in regulated sectors like healthcare and finance by offering auditing.

12. **Data Backup and Recovery**: RDBMSs have facilities for automated data backup and recovery, which lowers the chance of data loss due to hardware failures or user error.
13. **Transaction Processing**: Relational databases are frequently used in high-frequency transaction processing applications, including e-commerce, banking, and inventory management.
14. **Data Consistency in Applications:** They include techniques like foreign keys and referential integrity, which help maintain data quality and reliability, to assure data consistency in applications.
15. **Legacy Systems:** Relational databases are essential for maintaining and updating legacy systems because so many programs and systems now in use are built on them.

Thus, relational databases are essential for handling structured data, guaranteeing data integrity, facilitating data analysis, and enabling the effective operation of a variety of applications and businesses. It is impossible to exaggerate their importance in the fields of information technology and data management.

1.1. What Exactly Is a Computer Database?

An organisation's information is kept in the database in tables that are connected to each other. Tables are linked to each other in order to eliminate duplication and share data. A *relational database* is one that is managed using the relational model of data, treating it as a collection of tables. It has a collection of objects for managing, accessing, and storing data.

Tables, views, indexes, functions, triggers, and packages are a few examples of these types of objects. Objects can be defined by the user (user-defined objects) or by the system (built-in objects). A collection of tables and other items housed in a *distributed relational database* are dispersed over several linked but separate computer systems.

A relational database manager is built into every computer system to oversee the tables inside its surroundings. A particular database manager can run SQL statements on a different computer system thanks to the collaboration and communication between the database managers.

A relational database that has its data divided over several database partitions is called a *partitioned relational database*. The majority of SQL statements can see through this data separation between database partitions. Nonetheless, certain DDL (data definition language) statements—like CREATE DATABASE PARTITION GROUP—consider database partition information. The subset of SQL statements called DDL is used to specify the relationships between data in a database.

A relational database that has data saved in several different data sources—such as different relational databases—is called a *federated database*. Traditional SQL queries can access the data as if it were all contained in a single, sizable database. The right data source can be specifically referenced when making changes to the data.

1.2. Types of Computer Databases

According to the paradigm, there are three types of general databases:

- Relational Databases,
- Non-Relational Databases (NoSQL),
- Object-Oriented Databases

The way the data appears within the database distinguishes the models. As a result, the data linkages and management systems for each model type vary.

1. Relational Database

The most widely used and traditional database type is the *relational database model*. A relational database's three essential parts are:

- **Rows:** Examples or records of a certain kind of thing.
- **Columns:** Value the instance's characteristics.
- **Tables:** A kind of entity having relations.
  ### 1. Database Relationship Table Components

In answer to a query, a relational database returns a set of data rows. These data views are created with the aid of a query language, most frequently SQL, or Structured Query Language.

1. Features of Relational Databases

A relational database's primary characteristics are:

- **ACID conforming:** All of the data in the relational database is *consistent*. Relational databases that use integrity constraints (like rule enforcers) impose restrictions on data integrity, or the quality and completeness of the data that is now accessible.

- **Variety of Data Formats:** Allows for the storing of any data and the execution of sophisticated queries.
- **Collaborative:** The database can be accessed by multiple people who can collaborate on the same project.
- **Secure:** User permissions are used to restrict or limit access.
- **Stability:** Relational databases are extensively researched and understood. The completed transaction data is securely saved, even in the event of a system failure.

1. Why Would You Use a Relational Database?

The primary *advantage of a relational database* is its capacity to link data from several tables to produce insightful information. This method assists businesses of all sizes and sectors in identifying connections between disparate data sets from different departments in order to produce insightful analyses.

Numerous use cases exist, a few of them are as follows:

- **Data Warehouses:** Storage is a vital part of the architecture of the data warehouse. Relational databases are simple to integrate and are well-suited for large-scale queries coming from several sources.
- **Systems for Online Transactions:** Numerous users and the numerous queries required for online transactions are supported by the database.
- **Internet of Things (IoT):** Relational databases have the processing capability required for edge computing and are lightweight.

1. Top 10 Relational Databases in Use

There are innumerable open-source and commercial databases available. The ten most widely used relational databases are as follows:

- Oracle
- Azure SQL Database from Microsoft
- MySQL.
- Hive.
- SQL Server by Microsoft
- SQLite.
- Access from Microsoft
- PostgreSQL.
- IBM Db2
- MariaDB

1. **NoSQL Database (Non-Relational Database)**

Different from relational databases in how they model and store data is what's known as a *non-relational database*, or NoSQL ("Not Only SQL"). Non-relational databases use a different approach to model data relationships than tables do.

1. **Types of Non-Relational Databases**

Four types of NoSQL databases exist:

- Document
- Key-Value
- Column-based
- Graph
    1. **Features of Non-Relational Databases**

Non-relational databases include the following key characteristics:

- **Adaptable**: Non-relational database types make handling structured, semi-structured, and unstructured data easy.
- **Adaptable and Scalable.** Large data storage offers fast query

replies and scales effectively with on-demand servers.

- **Zero Downtime:** No idle time. Because data is replicated almost instantly, there is very little downtime and high availability.
- **Cloud Compatible:** Non-relational databases and cloud computing architectures combine seamlessly due to their scalability.
- **Multiple Data Structures.** There are various forms of information available, including multi-model database formats.

1. Why Would You Use a Non-Relational Database?

Large volumes of data and changeable data structures work best with non-relational databases. Among the use cases are:

- **Real-Time Systems:** The operational and analytical database systems are combined into one non-relational database. Non-relational databases offer the flexible real-time experience, whether they are used to serve analytics findings from Hadoop or to input operational data into it.
- **Personalised Experience:** Massive volumes of data are supported via elastic scalability for any personalized experience.
- **Detection of Fraud.** In order to detect fraud, high performance is essential. The low latency needs of financial systems are consistently met by non-relational databases, which are also responsive.

1. Top Non-Relational Databases in Use

The following are the top ten non-relational databases:

- Oracle NoSQL
- MySQL
- MongoDB
- Redis

- OrientDB
- CouchDB.
- Cassandra
- HBase
- Neo4j
- RavenDB
- Riak.

1. Object database

In object-oriented programming, an object database represents data in a similar way as objects. The following are essential elements of an object-oriented database:

- **Objects:** The fundamental components of an information storage system.
- **Classes:** The object's schema, or blueprint.
- **Techniques:** Class's structured habits.
- **Pointers:** Access database components and create relationships between items.

Object databases integrate database features with notions from object-oriented programming.

1. Features of Object Databases

Object databases' primary characteristics are:

- **ACID Transactions:** Because of ACID compliance, every transaction is finished and free of conflicts.
- **Transparency Persistence.** Object-oriented programming languages and object databases work together seamlessly.
- **Complex and Unique Data Types:** User-defined classes enable

the existence of complicated and custom data types.

- **Accessible:** Data is simple to store and get back.
- **Simplified Modeling.** Complex problems are easier to represent because real-world problems and information are more intimately tied to things.

1. Why Do We Use Object Databases?

Complex data types—where one entity contains a vast amount of information—are best suited for object databases. Typical applications for this kind of database model include:

- **High-Performance Software Programs:** Because data is saved and retrieved in its original form, object databases are advantageous for applications where quick data retrieval is essential.
- **For Scientific Reasons:** Both the mathematics and the data used in science are intricate. All branches of science benefit from the ability to store and retrieve large amounts of complex information quickly.
- **Complex Data Structures:** Reworking the database model is not necessary because database storage and complicated data expansion are available because objects have permanent persistence.

1. Top-Ranking Object Databases

The top ten object databases at the moment are:

- ObjectDatabase++
- Objectivity/DB
- Matisse
- DB4o
- ObjectStore
- Gemstone/S

"CAREERS IN INFORMATION TECHNOLOGY: DATABASE ADMINISTRATOR"

- Versant,
- Perst
- ObjectDB
- Jade

1.3. Database Types – Based on Location

Database types also vary according to where the storage is physically located.

Based on geography, the two groupings are:

1. Centralised Database systems
2. Distributed Database systems

1.3.1. Centralised Database system

A single location serves as both the storage and management of a consolidated database. A network provides access to the data. The centralized computer, which houses the stored data, is reachable by the end user via the network.

a. Features of Centralized Databases

A centralized database's primary characteristics are:

- **Data Integrity:** Reducing redundancy and maximizing data integrity are achieved by centralizing data. Reliability and correctness of the information are improved.
- **Security:** There is only one access point provided by a single point of location, which increases data security.
- **Friendly to End Users.** With a centralized database, updates and data access are instantaneous. The simplicity of a single database design is achieved.
- **Cost-Effectiveness:** A centralized system minimizes the need for personnel, electricity, and maintenance. From an administrative standpoint, the database is simpler to manage.
- **Data Preservation:** A configuration that is fault-tolerant thanks to disaster recovery tools.

a. Why Do We Use Centralized Databases?

Large institutions are the ones where the advantages of a centralized database are most apparent. Among the use cases are:

- **Management of Enterprises**: Centralized databases are used by large businesses to obtain a more comprehensive picture of all the data.
- **Official Data**. Government agencies frequently use centralized databases. Data security is ensured by one access point.
- **Universities and Schools**. Centralized databases are used by educational establishments. The information is reliable and the maintenance is economical.

1.3.2. Distributed Database

Information is stored in distributed databases at several physical locations. The database may be dispersed over several sites or housed on numerous CPUs at a single location. End users see the data as though it is contained in a single database because of the linkages between the dispersed databases.

a. Features of Distributed Databases

The following are a distributed database's most intriguing features:

- **Independence from Location**. The database is physically dispersed over several locations.
- **Distribution of query processing**. When a complicated query splits up into several sites, the workload is distributed across several CPUs, minimizing bottleneck.
- **Distributed Business Dealings**. A distributed recovery approach is made possible by many storage locations. There are commit protocols for multiple transactions.

- **Network Connection.** The distributed databases are connected by a network that facilitates communication with end users and between the storages.
- **Smooth Incorporation.** Distributed database components join into a single logical database even though they are not physically connected.

a. Why Would Someone Use a Distributed Database?

Distributed databases function best in multisector situations where businesses should restrict the amount of information they make available to cut down on redundancy.

Here are a few instances:

- **Big Businesses.** Most business sectors don't require a comprehensive data overview. Data redundancy with particular departments can be decreased with the use of distributed databases.
- **Worldwide Businesses**. Due to location independence, this database type fits well with companies with multiple sites.

1.3.4. Sorts of Databases by Design

The business goal determines how the storage is designed. There are two primary methods for designing databases:

1. A Transactional Or Operational Database
2. Analytical Database

Despite the fact that the databases have various functions, combining those results in a data warehouse system.

1. Operational (Transactional) Database

The core company operations are managed and controlled by an operational database. Online Transaction Processing, or OLTP, is the term used to describe the database. The information was gathered in real-time, straight from the source, and gave an overview of everyday transactions.

a. Features of Operational Databases

The characteristics of operational databases are as follows:

- **ACID Conforming**: Data organization requires maintaining each transaction's accuracy and integrity.
- **Speedy Processing.** Operational databases handle thousands of queries at once, thus processing them quickly is necessary.
- **Small Storage.** Transactional data is only kept in a transient state. Operational databases therefore act as a stopgap until the data is archived.
- **Regular Backups**. As data collection and storage necessitate continuous backups, legal compliance is a crucial component.

1. Analytical Database

A consolidated view of all the data accessible within a company is offered by analytical databases. A comprehensive overview of all the data in a database is necessary for decision-making, reporting, and planning. An online analytical processing (OLAP) database is what the database is called.

a. Features of Analytical Databases

Among an analytical database's characteristics are:

- **Distributed Workload**. The information is dispersed among nodes and originates from many operational systems.

- **Several Dimensions.** Data aggregation and sophisticated cross-database searches give enterprise information dimension.
- **Query Efficiency.** When performing time-consuming tasks, data denormalization enhances query efficiency.
- **Scaling Horizontally.** Scaling out analytical databases is necessary as an enterprise's needs increase.

1.3.5. Database Types according to Host

Databases can be hosted on several platforms. There are two locations where an information system can be found:

1. Databases hosted on-site (On-Premises)
2. Cloud Databases

The resources that are available at the time of the database deployment is the main distinction between the two approaches.

1. On-Premise Database

An internal or on-premise database is housed on-site. Every piece of infrastructure, software, and management required for support is local. Large businesses grow their storage to a nearby data center.

a. Features of On-premises Databases

On-premises database characteristics that are noteworthy are:

- **Security:** On-premises databases are the greatest option for storing sensitive data because of the internal infrastructure.
- **Control:** The organization maintains total control over the data that is accessible, offering a high degree of privacy and regulation.

- **Compliance:** HIPAA compliance and other regulatory controls necessitate knowing where sensitive data is located at all times.

1. **Cloud Database**

A hosting option provided by a third party is called a cloud database. By offering database-as-a-service, the pay-as-you-go option eliminates the need to physically set up a data center. The agile method rapidly expands as additional resources are needed while minimizing the initial expenses needed to obtain data space.

a. **Features of Cloud Databases**

A cloud database's best attributes are:

- **Scalability.** Cloud databases offer versatility. Virtualization enables rapid resource growth and decrease.
- **Flexibility in Management.** This kind of database is managed by the provider, which reduces the amount of client management required. On the other hand, maintenance outsourcing is an alternative.
- **Cost Efficiency:** You only pay for what you use when using a cloud database. Maintenance and hiring technical personnel come at the lowest possible cost.

1.3.6. Database Types According To Processor Capacity

The business model affects how the database is processed. Selecting the incorrect database system tier has an impact on an organization's and team's workflow. The majority of database suppliers provide a variety of database processing options.

The primary two are:

1. Personal (Individual) Database
2. Commercial (Business-related) Database

Depending on the use case, businesses combine the strengths of the two.

1. Personal (Individual) Database

Personal databases run on low- to medium-powered computers and provide single-user access. This database type's minimal cost and maintenance make it ideal for simpler database applications.

1. Commercial (Business-Related) Database

A business database has many programs running on powerful computers and multiple users with different rights. Commercial databases with high availability are expensive and require ongoing support and maintenance.

1.4. Crucial Terminologies in Database Administration

When talking about Database Administration, it's helpful to know the following terms:

a. **Tables:** A relational database's basic building block is a table. They are made up of columns and rows. Every table represents a certain entity or kind of information, such as clients, orders, goods, personnel, etc. In a table, the rows stand in for specific records or instances of data, while the columns represent the qualities or characteristics of those entries.

b. **Records and Rows**: Records, sometimes referred to as tuples or rows, house the actual data entries. A table's rows each represent a single data entity or record. For instance, every row in a "Customers" table can correspond to a different client.

c. **Columns and Attributes:** A table's columns and attributes specify the kinds of data that can be stored inside. A specific attribute or property of the data items is represented by one or more columns. For instance, you might have columns for "CustomerID," "FirstName," "LastName," "Email," and so on in a "Customers" database.

d. **Primary Key:** A primary key is a number that uniquely identifies every record in a table. It guarantees that every row has a distinct identity. Customer IDs, product IDs, or social security numbers are examples of frequently used primary keys.

e. **Foreign Key**: A foreign key is a column that connects the primary key of one table to another table's primary key. In order to link related data from several tables together, this connection is employed. An "Orders" table, for instance, may have a foreign key connecting it to the "Customers" table.

f. **Table Relationships:** The connections between main and foreign keys define the connections between tables. One-to-one, one-to-many, and many-to-many connections are frequent types of relationships.

g. **SQL (Structured Query Language):** The standard language for interacting with relational databases is SQL (Structured Query Language). Users can query, insert, update, and delete data, among other activities, with this tool.

h. **Data Integrity Constraints:** Relational databases use constraints to protect data integrity, such as check constraints, referential integrity constraints, and uniqueness requirements. These limitations aid in maintaining the consistency and accuracy of the data in the database.

i. **ACID Properties:** Relational databases are renowned for supporting the ACID qualities (Atomicity, Consistency, Isolation, Durability), which ensure that database transactions are trustworthy and uphold data integrity.

j. **Normalization:** To lessen redundancy and increase data integrity, normalization is the act of structuring data in a database. To avoid duplicate data, it entails splitting up big tables into smaller, relevant ones.

k. **Indexes:** Data structures called indexes are used to speed up data retrieval procedures. They provide quicker data retrieval and searches based on particular columns.

l. **Designing Databases:** When you design a database, you are simulating an actual business system with a collection of entities, their attributes, and the rules or connections that bind them together.

m. **Establishing Databases:** The build DATABASE command is used to build a database. Use the sqlecrea API to construct a database from a client application. Unless otherwise specified, all databases are built with the IBMSTOGROUP default storage group. Self-storing automata Storage groups are used by managed table spaces to define their storage.

n. **Buffer Pools:** The database manager has set aside a portion of main memory called a buffer pool to be used as a cache for table and index data that is read from disk. There must be a buffer pool in every Db2 database.

o. **Looking At The Files In The System Or Local Database Directory:** To see the details related to the databases you have on your system, use the LIST DATABASE DIRECTORY command.

p. **Partitioning In Databases:** A portion of a database with its own data, indexes, configuration files, and transaction logs is called a database partition. A node or database node are other terms for a database division. A database installation that permits data distribution among database partitions is known as a partitioned database environment.

q. **Linking Up With Distributed Relational Databases:** The foundation of distributed relational databases is formal requester-server functions and protocols.

r. **Storage Groups:** A storage group consists of a designated collection of storage pathways for data storage. Storage groups are set up to symbolize the various storage types that your database system has access to. Table slots can be allocated to the storage group that best accommodates the data. Storage groups are only used by automatic storage table spaces.

s. **Table Spaces:** A table space is a type of storage structure that holds long data, huge objects, tables, and indexes. They serve the purpose of arranging database data into logical storage groupings that correspond to the locations of data on a system. Database partition groups are used to store table spaces.

t. **Dropping Databases:** Because dropping a database also deletes all of its related files, containers, and objects, the consequences of this operation can be extensive. From the database directories, the discarded database is eliminated (un-cataloged).

u. **Schemas:** A schema is an ordered set of named items that offers a logical manner to put the things together. In addition to serving as a name qualifier, a schema also allows for the use of one natural name for several objects while avoiding confusing references to those objects.

Because they can store structured data, create relationships between data elements, and offer robust querying capabilities, relational databases are widely utilized in many applications and sectors. They are crucial tools for effectively managing and organizing data.

a. Database Architecture

A *database architecture* is a DBMS design representation. It supports the database management system's creation, development, implementation, and upkeep. The database system can be divided into separate components that can be independently changed, replaced, and adjusted thanks to a DBMS design.

The management of data, from collection to transformation, dissemination, and consumption, is outlined in a *data architecture*. It establishes the guidelines for data and how it moves across systems for storing data. Artificial intelligence (AI) applications and data processing activities both rely on it. Business requirements should guide the design of a data architecture, since they are used by data architects and data engineers to specify the corresponding data model and supporting data structures. Usually, these designs serve a business purpose, such reporting or data science projects.

Emerging technologies like the Internet of Things (IoT) give rise to new data sources, but a sound data architecture makes sure that data is manageable and usable, supporting data lifecycle management. More precisely, it can prevent redundant data storage, facilitate the creation of new applications, and enhance data quality through deduplication and cleansing. In addition, contemporary data architectures offer ways to break down data silos by integrating data across departments, regions, and other domains without adding to the enormous complexity that comes with centrally storing all of the data.

Cloud platforms are frequently used in modern data infrastructures for data processing and management. Important data processing activities can be finished quickly thanks to its computing scalability, despite the fact that it can be more expensive. Scalable storage also makes it easier to handle growing data volumes and guarantees that all pertinent data is accessible to enhance the calibre of AI training programs.

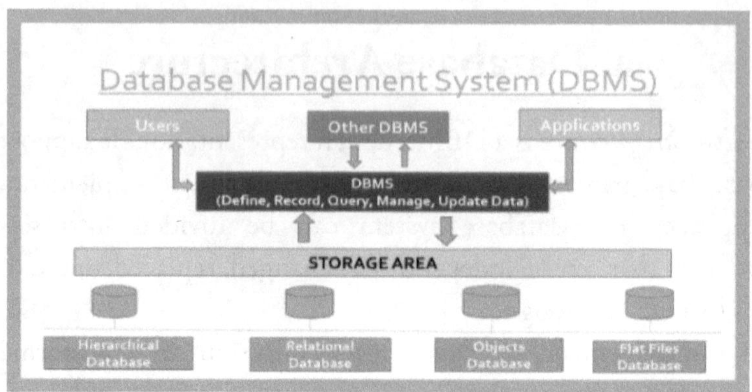

Figure 1: Database Management System (DBMS), Copyright: Patrick Mukosha (2023),

Source: "Mastering Relational Databases: *From Fundamentals to Advanced Concepts*"

b. Database Security

The procedures, equipment, and controls that safeguard databases from unintentional and deliberate attacks are together referred to as *database security*. Protecting sensitive data and preserving the database's availability, confidentiality, and integrity are the goals of database security.

The term "*database security*" describes the assortment of instruments, regulations, and protocols intended to create and maintain the confidentiality, integrity, and accessibility of databases. Since confidentiality is typically breached in data breaches, it will be the main topic of discussion in this article.

The following must be addressed and safeguarded by database security:

- The network and/or computer system required to access the database
- Every related application
- The database's contents
- The system for managing databases (DBMS)
- The underlying hardware, the virtual database server, or the physical database server

Database security encompasses all facets of information security technologies and procedures, making it a difficult and complex undertaking. A database's susceptibility to security threats increases with its accessibility and usability; conversely, a database's resistance to threats decreases with its difficulty of access and usage.

Chapter 2: Understanding the Database Administration

The task of overseeing and preserving database management systems (DBMS) software is known as *Database Administration*. Regular maintenance is required for mainstream DBMS software like Microsoft SQL Server, IBM Db2, and Oracle. Because of this, businesses that utilize DBMS software frequently employ *Database Administrators,* or DBAs, who are specialists in information technology.

2.1. What exactly is Database Administration?

The entire range of tasks carried out by a database administrator to guarantee that a database is always accessible when needed is referred to as *Database Administration*. Planning for future expansion, database monitoring and troubleshooting, and database security are additional duties and positions that are closely related. Therefore, any company that relies on one or more databases must do database administration.

In *large enterprises*, the database administrator (DBA) typically holds a specialized position inside the IT department. Nonetheless, a lot of *smaller businesses* who can't afford a full-time DBA typically contract or outsource the job to a specialist vendor, combine it with another ICT department job, or have one employee do both.

Ensuring maximum database uptime is the main responsibility of database administrators in order to guarantee that the database is always accessible when needed. Usually, this will entail proactive, recurring monitoring and troubleshooting. Thus, the DBA needs to possess a few technical abilities. The DBA will require expertise in the platform (database engine and operating system) in addition to in-depth understanding of the database in question.

Typically, a DBA is also in charge of additional jobs and duties that are less important but yet very crucial. A few of these consist of:

- *Database security* is protecting the database from external, unauthorized access and making sure that only authorized users have access to it.
- *Database tuning* is the process of adjusting many parameters, including disk utilization, file fragmentation, and server memory allocation, to maximize performance.
- *Backup and Recovery*: A DBA's responsibility is to guarantee that the database has sufficient backup and recovery protocols

set up so that any unintentional or intentional data loss may be recovered from.

- *Creating Reports from Queries:* Creating reports is a common task for DBAs. They do this by writing queries and running them against the database.

From everything mentioned above, it is evident that *years of expertise* and *technical knowledge* are necessary for the database management role. A few businesses that sell commercial database products, including Microsoft SQL Server and Oracle DB, also provide certifications for the particular systems they sell. A DBA's extensive training on the product in issue is mostly guaranteed by these industry certifications, such as Microsoft Certified Database Administrator (MCDBA) and Oracle Certified Professional (OCP). Today's DBAs will find it beneficial to have a working knowledge of SQL syntax and instructions, as the majority of relational database solutions employ this language.

2.2. Who is a Database Administrator?

A *Database Administrator*, or DBA, is responsible for maintaining, securing, and operating databases and also ensures that data is correctly stored and retrieved. In addition, DBAs often work with developers to design and implement new features and troubleshoot any issues. A DBA must have a strong understanding of both technical and business needs.

The role of DBA is becoming increasingly important in today's information-driven business environment. Throughout the world, more and more organizations depend on data to discover analytical insights on market conditions, new business models, and cost-cutting measures. The global cloud computing market is also expected to expand as companies move their business operations to the cloud. Consequently, the need for qualified DBAs will only continue to grow.

The specific responsibilities of a database administrator *vary depending on the size and needs of the organization* they work for. However, most DBA duties will include developing and maintaining databases, ensuring data security, tuning performance, backing up data, and providing training and support to users. DBAs may also be responsible for designing databases and overseeing their construction in larger organizations.

2.3. Database Administrators: What Do They Do?

An organization's database maintenance and data security are the responsibilities of a *Database Administrator* (DBA), a specialist in computer systems administration. Preserving data integrity, ensuring user access, and averting unwanted access are top priorities for a DBA. They are in charge of *comprehending and overseeing* the entire database environment. When necessary, they also upgrade, test, and make adjustments to the database. Assuming a DBA position requires addressing complicated problems, therefore having a love for solving problems is crucial.

Although many DBAs handle databases in a generic capacity, some have specific areas of expertise that they tailor to the demands of the company they work for.

A database administrator may be in charge of many different tasks pertaining to the upkeep and management of a database system. Depending on the size of their department, database administrators may not finish these jobs to the same degree.

A database administrator's typical responsibilities include:

- Database server software installation, configuration, and upgrade, as well as associated goods.
- Perform general technological debugging and provide drawbacks.
- Performance tracking and database tweaking.
- Performance tracking and application tweaking.
- Analyze database features and goods associated with databases.
- Collaborate as a group and offer round-the-clock assistance when needed.
- Database Recovery / Restoration.
- Create and follow reliable policies and procedures for backup

and recovery.

- Attend to the design and implementation of the database.
- Establish and manage database security (assign privileges, create and manage roles and users).
- Establish and preserve standards and documentation.
- Prepare for changes and expansion (capacity planning).

2.4. Types of Database Administrators

There are various kinds of database administrators, and each has distinct responsibilities and tasks.

Three categories of DBAs exist:

a. **Systems DBA:** The physical aspects of database administration, such as DBMS installation, configuration, patching, upgrades, backups, restores, refreshes, performance optimization, maintenance, and disaster recovery, are the focus of systems DBAs, also known as physical DBAs, operations DBAs, or production Support DBAs. Typically with a background in system architecture, these database administrators manage the technical and structural elements of a database. They do out duties like applying updates or patches to address software issues.

b. **Development Database Administrators (DBAs):** Concentrate on the logical and development aspects of database administration, including the creation and upkeep of data models, the writing and tuning of SQL, the coding of stored procedures, working with developers to select the best DBMS features and functionalities, and other pre-production tasks. Are in charge of creating the digital framework that businesses can use to construct their database systems. The efficient use of database resources is made possible by well-designed database architecture.

c. **Application DBAs** - These database managers provide support for databases created especially for particular uses, including computer services. This kind of DBA can develop code or debug it; to fix issues with an application, they frequently employ sophisticated programming languages. Application DBAs are typically employed by companies that have purchased third-party application software, such as CRM (customer relationship management) and ERP (enterprise resource planning) programs. Oracle Applications, SAP, Siebel and PeopleSoft (now owned by Oracle Corp.), and Oracle Applications are a few examples of this type of application software. Application DBAs are in charge of making sure that the application is fully optimized for the database and vice versa, sitting on the fence between the DBMS and the application software. Typically, they oversee every application component that communicates with the database and perform tasks including database cloning, application upgrades, installation and patching, data load process management, and designing and executing data cleanup routines.

Although people typically specialize in one area of database administration, it is not unusual to find a single person or group handling multiple aspects of database administration in smaller businesses.

However, for large organisations, these broad DBA types can be *broken down further* - depending on their job roles as follows:

System administrators, database architects, database analysts, data modellers, application DBAs, task-oriented DBAs, performance analysts, data warehouse administrators, and cloud DBAs are among the most prevalent kinds of DBAs.

a. **System Administrators** - Are in charge of managing a computer system's overall configuration, installing and configuring software, updating security patches, and keeping an eye on the system's performance.

b. **Database Architects** - Create databases that specifically address an organization's needs.

c. **Database Analysts** - Data is gathered and examined by database analysts to enhance database efficiency. They could also be in charge of creating reports and giving database administrators advice.

- **Data Modellers** - Data models that show the relationships between data items are created and maintained by data modellers. A vital part of a successful database architecture is data modelling.
- **Database administration** - For apps is the responsibility of application DBAs. Applications must be installed and configured, data synchronization between databases must be checked, and application-related problems must be trouble-shooted.
- **Task-Oriented DBAs** - Concentrate on certain aspects of database management, like security, performance optimization, and backup and recovery. Usually, they are extremely knowledgeable about a particular *Database Management System* (DBMS).
- **Performance Analysts** - keep an eye on database performance and pinpoint areas in need of development. They could also be in charge of writing performance reports and advising database administrators.
- **Data Warehouse Administrators** - Databases used to store data for business intelligence and decision-support applications are managed by data warehouse administrators. Correct data extraction, transformation, and data warehouse loading are their responsibilities.

In addition to deploying and managing database instances, setting up replication and high availability, and keeping an eye on database performance, cloud DBAs are in charge of administering databases housed in cloud computing environments.

2.5. What Does a Database Administrator's Ordinary Day Entail?

Typically, database administration is a typical job with set business hours. It is common for database administrators to work *40 hours a week* concurrently with other employees. They could also be in charge of emergency responses.

In the event that a mistake occurs in the company's database system that needs to be fixed right away in order to avoid a delay in the following workday, a database administrator may be required to work during non-business hours.

Once they have determined user needs and set up databases with appropriate disk space, network requirements, and memory, database administrators may spend their days using software tools to organize and store company records, user information, and other data.

Other daily tasks include:

- Upgrading database servers and applications,
- Modifying database structure as needed,
- Generating user profiles, and
- Monitoring database security.

2.6. Which Competencies Are Required to Work as a Database Administrator?

Database administrators, like many other scientific and technological professionals, must acquire and use a number of hard skills in order to do their work. The following challenging talents must be learned through patience, focus, and technological aptitude. Remember that the particular hard skills needed for database management differ depending on the organization, role, and project.

a. **Crucial Hard Skills**

- **Windows Operating System:** Windows OS is the graphical user interface that serves as the foundation for all Microsoft products. Unlike Linux and UNIX systems, Windows—the fundamental operating system for Microsoft desktops and applications—is controlled by a corporation and is not publicly available. Windows OS is currently the most used operating system globally.
- **UNIX:** The Open Group provides this multiuser, portable, multitasking operating system interface. UNIX, which is written in the C programming language, serves as the structural basis for the majority of Mac, Android, Chrome, and PlayStation systems. As such, it serves as a fundamental component of database administration and management.
- **Linux:** Based on the UNIX operating system, this open-source operating system is flexible enough to run a wide range of computing devices, from supercomputers to smartphones. Installing Linux is free, and users can construct full platforms for customers and businesses by using online coding and troubleshooting hacks.
- **SQL:** All data management systems are oriented and organized

using SQL, a computer language. The three most common database languages should be understood by students: IBM's DB2, Oracle Database, and Microsoft SQL. It may be necessary for professionals to use MySQL for website development, Transact-SQL for relational database creation, and PL/SQL for object-oriented concept control.

- **HTML:** Hypertext Markup Language, sometimes known as HTML, is used to create platform and website design visuals. Professionals use this common coding language, which incorporates scripting languages like JavaScript, to develop interactive systems and webpages. Because HTML is the foundation of computer programming, database managers need to be familiar with it.

- **Microsoft Access:** The primary information management tool used in data administration for reference, reporting, and data analysis is Microsoft Access. MS Access converts metadata collections into useable, searchable datasets, especially from Microsoft Excel sheets. This tool is used by database managers to group materials together and emphasize relationships across datasets.

- **Oracle:** Oracle is a relational database framework that organizes and grants access to datasets via SQL. Additionally, it incorporates data into platforms that businesses and organizations may easily use. Like SQL, Oracle is compatible with the majority of important platforms.

- **Data Analysis:** Data analysts turn vast amounts of information into relevant and illustrative content for businesses and clients by examining, compiling, and analyzing datasets. Additionally, analysts employ analytical interpretation to increase system efficiency by cleaning datasets, which includes itemizing and prioritizing metadata, and by offering suggestions for system enhancements.

a. Crucial Soft Skills

Additionally, database administrators need to have a few all-around, less-measurable abilities and talents, or "soft skills." Problem-solving, organizing, and communication skills are beneficial in practically every role. Candidates with analytics and business acumen are especially valued by companies that make data-driven judgments.

- **Communication:** As database administrators frequently oversee other IT personnel, effective communication is essential to IT leadership and teamwork. Database administrators converse with vendors, other firms' technology experts, and upper management as well.
- **Problem-Solving**: Database administrators spend a lot of time troubleshooting, thus the ability to recognize, test, and eradicate potential problems and their causes is quite valuable. Additionally, as database administrators frequently have to come up with novel answers to fresh challenges, creativity is required.
- **Organisation**: Database administrators organize data in order to make database choices and generate reports. Databases require a great deal of organization. They also arrange the work and personnel of the IT department.
- **Analytics:** The capacity to methodically examine data or statistics aids database administrators in determining and satisfying the data management requirements of their organizations. Additionally, database managers frequently perform updated analyses of their databases.
- **Business-Focused:** Organizations rely on database administrators to make economical choices about personnel and technology for data analysis, security, maintenance, and storage. Database administrators are more valuable and adaptable when they possess both technical and commercial

knowledge and abilities.

2.7. Typical levels of competencies needed for different types of Database Administrators (DBAs)

"CAREERS IN INFORMATION TECHNOLOGY: DATABASE ADMINISTRATOR"

BDA Type	Competency	Entry-Level Competencies	Mid-Level Competencies	Senior-Level Competencies
Database Administrator	Database Concepts	Understanding of relational databases	Proficiency in one or more DBMS (e.g., MySQL, PostgreSQL)	Expertise in multiple DBMS, including optimization
	Databases	Basic SQL knowledge	Advanced SQL skills	In-depth knowledge of SQL and query optimization
	Disaster Recovery	Familiarity with data backup and recovery procedures	Performance tuning and optimization skills	Disaster recovery planning and execution expertise
	Security	Security and access control basics	High-level security and access control proficiency	- Security auditing and compliance expertise
	Monitoring & Evaluation	Monitoring and troubleshooting skills	Advanced monitoring tools usage	Proactive performance monitoring and tuning
	Programming	Basic scripting/ automation skills	Scripting and automation expertise	Advanced scripting/ automation for routine tasks
	Documentation	Documentation and reporting abilities	Documentation and reporting improvements	Process optimization and best practices documentation
	Database	Understanding of	Design and	- Expertise in

Architecture	database architecture	implement high-availability solutions	database architecture ar scaling
Backup and Recovery	Knowledge of basic disaster recovery concepts	Implementing disaster recovery solutions	Disaster recove planning, testi and continuou improvement
Migration	Familiarity with database migration and upgrade processes	Execute migrations and upgrades	Lead complex migration and upgrade projec
Troubleshooting	Basic troubleshooting skills for database issues	Complex issue diagnosis and resolution	Mentorship an guidance for junior DBAs
Communication	Collaborative skills for working with development teams	Effective communication and collaboration with stakeholders	Strategic planning and database road-mapping

Copyright: Patrick Mukosha (2023),

Typical levels of competencies needed for different types of Database Administrators (DBAs)

Source: "Careers in ICT: *Database Administrator*"

Figure 1: Typical levels of competencies needed for different types of Database Administrators (DBAs)

Note: This table outlines the typical competencies required at various stages of a Database Administrator's career, from entry-level to mid-level, and senior-level positions. Keep in mind that the specific skills and expertise needed may vary depending on the organization and the particular database management systems in use

2.8. How to Get Ready for an Interview in Database Administration

You might research possible interview questions online and develop compelling responses in order to better prepare for your database administration interview. Study up on the company you want to work for as well as how they handle interviews.

Example questions for a Database Administration Interview:

- Do you have any practical experience with cloud databases, on-premises Databases?
- Which kinds of databases are in use at this time?
- How many database servers have you worked with most recently?
- If you were migrating a database, how would you handle losing data?

Chapter 3: A Career in Database Administration

Degree programs in database administration provide students with the fundamental information and abilities needed for a variety of IT and computer science jobs. While most network architects, computer programmers, and software developers require bachelor's degrees along with relevant certifications and work experience, computer systems analysts with the necessary programming skills can occasionally find employment with just an associate's degree. Master's degrees may also be necessary for professionals in managerial positions at big businesses.

These pointers could assist you in honing your abilities and becoming ready for the database administration field if you're interested in a career in that field:

3.1. 4 Easy Steps for Database Administrator Career

You can take the following actions to pursue a profession in *Database Administration*:

1. **Get your Degree:** Most businesses prefer individuals with a bachelor's degree in a computer-related subject, however others will consider applicants with an associate's degree. Look for available Database administrator jobs nearby and find out what kind of schooling is needed for those opportunities. You might then seek for a course of study that will equip you for this line of work. Hard skills are essential for IT professions and can be developed by applicants via online learning resources and independent study. However, the majority of jobs also call for a bachelor's degree in CS or IT. Database management and administration are two of the concentrations available in several IT bachelor's degree programs.

Through courses on data structures, network architecture, web programming, and software applications, these programs educate students computer programming languages such as Python, HTML5, CSS, and C++. To graduate from many programs, students must complete a capstone project or an internship. Job seekers with bachelor's degrees may need to obtain extra certifications in particular database systems or software programs by Microsoft, IBM, Oracle, Altibase, and other companies because database systems management and software programs differ by employer.

1. **Gain Experience:** In order to work as database administrators, candidates must have prior experience in the field and in a

relevant role. Consequently, bachelor's degrees that combine IT internships and/or portfolio capstone projects are generally advantageous for prospective database administrators. Through these channels, students can become developers or systems administrators in the IT field, and individuals who succeed in these roles are more likely to be hired as database administrators.

While certain positions may have different hard skill requirements, entry-level database administrators frequently need knowledge of Oracle, IBMDB2, Altibase, SQL, and SAP Sybase ASE as well as database administration and reporting. Professionals with four or more years of experience, additional credentials, and proficiency in data analysis are required for mid-level database administrator roles. Taking up database management Students might benefit from student chapters or networking clubs offered by professional associations or educational initiatives.

1. **Obtain Vendor Certifications:** Depending on the particular products they use, system and network administrators might need to obtain certifications. When an administrator works with vendors like Microsoft or Oracle, it's typical for them to demand certification from the vendor to guarantee they have the necessary skills for fixing their equipment. The vendors will provide these credentials, and after an applicant is hired, the employer might mandate that the candidate obtain one of these certifications. Employers typically prefer applicants with a mix of vendor and non-vendor certifications. These certifications validate the skill set of the IT specialist and provide in-depth understanding of the software used by the company. To demonstrate to prospective employers your willingness to develop, learn, and advance in your position quickly, think

about earning certifications.

1. **Obtain Certification:** Database administration-focused associate's and bachelor's degree programs cover programming languages, pertinent software, and systems management courses. However, some individuals who want to work as database administrators could require more formal certificates. For instance, candidates holding ordinary bachelor's degrees in IT or computer science might require further database administrator certification.

Thankfully, job seekers have the option to obtain effective professional certificates at different levels of specialization that are centered on their needs and goals for their careers. Microsoft, for instance, certifies users in SQL Server at the entry, associate, and advanced levels. IBM offers an intermediate database administrator certification for Linux, UNIX, and Windows, while Oracle offers certificates for databases and MySQL at multiple levels. Typically, certification programs consist of multiple courses or modules that end with one or more tests.

3.2. Educational Pathways

The degree of education needed to become a network administrator varies depending on the company. Most, however, would demand at least an associate's degree in a field linked to computers in addition to any necessary certifications. Nonetheless, a bachelor's degree in computer technology, network engineering, security, or a similar field of study is sometimes required by employers for network administrators. You will learn about web development, cloud foundations, data management, scripting and programming languages, Linux, and more in these study topics.

3.3. Training

The majority of the necessary training is available through both traditional schooling and on-the-job training. While you're getting your bachelor's degree, look into internships in IT departments to gain real-world experience. Students can make relationships with IT professionals who can assist them in finding careers after graduating from college in addition to receiving practical experience. Before applying, it's critical to read job descriptions to determine the level of training required for the position.

3.4. Certification Levels for Database Administrators

While most IT professions require a bachelor's degree in database administration, computer science (CS), management information systems, or a similar discipline, some entry-level data occupations may accept people with associate degrees in database administration.

Additional professional credentials are usually needed for more advanced employment.

No matter what academic path you choose, becoming proficient in SQL is essential for DBAs. The language known as SQL is used to query data kept in relational databases. Among other businesses, the finance and marketing sectors frequently utilize it, and our Learn SQL course will teach you how to use it.

However, not all businesses employ relational databases. Since NoSQL (not-only-SQL) databases provide more flexibility and scalability, more people prefer to utilize them. For this reason, DBAs also need to be certified with technologies like MongoDB, which we cover in our Learn MongoDB course.

5.1.3 14 Certifications in Database Administration

Your initial position as a DBA will probably still be entry-level even if you have a specialist degree. It will take less time to land a higher-level DBA position if you supplement your academic background with certifications, training, and programming language proficiency. A master's degree in a relevant discipline is probably required for DBA positions at the managerial level.

The specifications and explanations of the fourteen database administrator certifications are provided below:

S/N	Certification	Details
1	**Microsoft Certified Azure Fundamentals**	This is intended to give novices a basic understanding of Azure databases. • Pre-requisite: Basic awareness of data workloads and concepts, such as relational and non-relational data, before starting the certification program. • A lot of participants prepare for this certification process over the course of several weeks or months. • The actual exam lasts for ninety minutes.
2	**Microsoft Certified Azure Database Administrator Associate**	This certification proves that database managers are proficient in building a High Availability and Disaster Recovery (HADR) environment, automating database processes, and allocating data resources appropriately.

- Either enrolling in one of Microsoft's free online training courses or paying for an instructor-led program can help participants get ready for this certification exam.

For those who are interested in working with NoSQL or non-relational databases or who are currently employed in such environments, this certification may be useful.

3   **MongoDB Associate Database Administrator**

- Essential database and server administration concepts, software development, and systems programming are taught to participants in the certification program.
- MongoDB provides online practice questions and study materials, and anyone can register to take the exam.
- Participants get 90

minutes to complete the 60 multiple-choice questions on the qualifying exam.

The IBM Data Analyst Professional Certificate equips candidates for data analytics entry-level jobs.

4

IBM Data Analyst Professional Certificate

- This credential demonstrates the ability to use a variety of analytical methodologies to a wide range of data sets, create data visualizations, and communicate research findings to others.
- To obtain the credential, you must first register for and complete eight complimentary courses provided by IBM, after which you must pass the related tests that gauge your grasp of important ideas.

Vantage Data Science Master

5

With this expert-level certification, a database administrator may show that they have extensive understanding of designing and managing Teradata enterprise-wide data warehouses.

- Having the abilities to design, deploy, assess, and oversee these systems at every stage of the data warehouse development process is part of this.
- Teradata expects candidates to get the Vantage Analytics, Vantage Data Science, and Vantage Data Engineering certificates prior to obtaining the Vantage Data Science Master credential.

PostgreSQL Associate Certification

6

The certification proves principles of PostgreSQL, an object-relational database system that is open-source.

- The system's configuration,

implementation, and upkeep are included in these foundations.

- In order to obtain this certification, candidates must pass an hour-long multiple-choice exam, which can be taken online.

- As a requirement, EnterpriseDB, the company that offers the certification, suggests taking the Foundations of PostgreSQL course.

This certification attests to candidates' mastery of fundamental database concepts.

7

SAP Certified Application Associate, Reporting, Modeling, Data Acquisition, and Using SAP BW/ 4HANA 2.x

- Participants gain a basic understanding of modeling, data collecting, and query creation with SAP BW/ 4HANA. The exam lasts 180 minutes and has 80 questions. A minimum of 65% or above is required for passing.

An experienced database administrator can obtain the IBM Certified Administrator - Netezza Performance Server V11.x accreditation. This certification shows that a person is proficient with the IBM Netezza Performance Server.

8

IBM Certified Administrator - Netezza Performance Server V11.x

- The certification program covers architecture, related best practices, system management, and supportive tools for this performance server.
- This 90-minute test requires a minimum of 41 correct answers out of 60 questions to pass.

The MongoDB Developer Certification program can help database administrators improve their skills, even though it is more focused on developer skill sets.

9

MongoDB Associate Developer Certification

- You have the option to become certified in a variety of languages and environments, including C#, Python, and Node.js, for MongoDB skills.

- The management and entry of information and documents into databases is covered in this certification program.
- There are 53 multiple-choice questions on the test.

The extract, transform, and load (ETL) data process is the main topic of the 4.2 certificate.

10	**SAP Certified Application Associate: Data Integration SAP Services 4.22**	<ul><li>Participants learn how to use SAP Data Services and execute ETL projects, including troubleshooting exercises and performance design optimization.</li><li>In the 180 minutes allotted for the exam, candidates respond to 80 questions.</li></ul>
11	**IBM Certified Specialist**	This is a certification for users of

IBM's InfoSphere Optim data management products at the intermediate level.

- InfoSphere Optim for Distributed Systems Fundamentals

- Participants learn how to install, set up, generate, manage, and privatize data in an InfoSphere Optim environment.
- IBM requires candidates to correctly answer at least 41 out of 60 questions in a 90-minute allotment of time in order to pass the test and obtain the certification.

Participants learn how to handle, install, configure, and troubleshoot various databases.

Apache Cassandra Administrator Associate Certificate

- You can take online courses from DataStax at any time using a secure digital platform to get ready for the certification exam.
- 70% of the questions in the 90-minute exam must be answered

12

correctly to succeed

Your capacity to review, evaluate, and derive conclusions from data of various kinds using research, analytical abilities, and technical knowledge is put to the test in this program.
The following certification levels are your options:

- **Executive Management**: To reach this level, one must pass a test with a minimum score of 70% and finish a four-day training program.
- **Principal:** To advance to this level, you must finish a two-day workshop and receive at least 70% on three tests.
- **Mastery:** To reach this level, you must receive at least 70% on three exams.
- **Associate/ Practitioner:** Three exam scores of at least 50% are needed to

13   ICCP Certified Data Scientist

advance to this level.

- **Basic:** Two exam scores of at least 50% are needed to advance to this level.

Depending on your choice, tests can take anywhere from 60 to 90 minutes to complete. Four to five years of technical expertise are necessary to get top certification levels.

You have the option of concentrating on data and information quality, data warehousing, analytics, and design.

Moreover, you can pursue any one of the following five certification levels based on your interests, ambitions, and level of competence:

- **Executive Management:** This position needs passing a test with a minimum score of 70% and completing a four-day training program.
- **Principal:** To advance

Certified Data Professional (ICCP)

14

to this level, you must finish a two-day workshop and receive at least 70% on three tests.

- **Mastery:** To reach this level, you must receive at least 70% on three exams.

- **Associate/ Practitioner:** Three exam scores of at least 50% are needed to advance to this level.

- **Basic:** Two exam scores of at least 50% are needed to advance to this level.

Depending on the certification level you choose to pursue, testing periods can last anywhere from 60 to 90 minutes. Different certificates have different requirements.

Copyright: Patrick Mukosha (2023),
Type of Certifications for Database Administrators (DBAs)
Source: "Careers in ICT: *Database Administrator*"
Figure 2: Type of Certifications for Database Administrators (DBAs)

"CAREERS IN INFORMATION TECHNOLOGY: DATABASE ADMINISTRATOR"

Note: The demand for data analysis and management is expected to expand significantly in the future, which bodes well for DBA qualifications. DBA credentials are becoming a necessary tool for job searchers to differentiate themselves in a crowded market.

Chapter 4: Roles & Responsibilities of a Database Administrator

4.1. What Is The Work Of a Database Administrator?

A DBA's routine tasks, as described in ITIL® Service Operation, consist of the following:

- Defining and putting into practice event triggers to notify users of possible problems with database integrity or performance.
- Monitoring database performance and availability, including incident and problem handling.
- Keeping an eye on things like concurrency levels, response times, transaction volumes, and use.
- Establishing and upholding policies and standards for databases.
- Supporting the design, development, and testing of databases.
- Managing database objects to attain maximum efficiency.
- Carrying out housekeeping tasks for databases, like indexing and tweaking.
- Recognizing and handling database security vulnerabilities, audit trails, and forensics.
- Creating a strategy for database preservation, backup, and storage system.

4.2. Database Administrators' Work Environment

Database administrators and architects work in nearly all industries. For example, in retail they may design databases that track buyers' shipping information; in healthcare, they may manage databases that secure patients' medical records.

Many database architects and administrators work for companies that offer computer design services or for organizations that have big databases, such insurance and educational institutions. Most architects and database administrators are full-time employees.

Chapter 5: Salary Scales of Database Administrator

5.1. What Is The Salary Of A Database Administrator?

A database administrator typically makes $90,640 a year. A database administrator's pay is determined by a number of factors, such as employer size and prominence, education level, and experience.

When accepting a contract for a database administrator role, having negotiating abilities may help you boost the size of your salary package.

Chapter 6: Areas of Specialisation

6.1. How May DDA Focus on A Particular Area of Work?

If you're interested in a career in data, there's a good chance you'll use relational databases at some point.

These five roles include:

1. **Database Administrator**: database administrators perform backups, data migrations, and load balancing in addition to acting as technical support for databases.
2. **Data Engineer**: data engineers design and build systems for data collection and analysis. They typically use SQL to query relational databases to manage the data and look for inconsistencies or patterns that may positively or negatively affect an organization's goals.
3. **Data Architect:** To plan or implement databases and database management systems that increase workflow efficiency, data architects examine the data infrastructure of a business.
4. **Data Analyst**: To answer a business query or issue, data analysts extract, clean, and interpret data sets from relational databases. They can be employed in a wide range of fields, including government, research, finance, and business.
5. **Data Scientist:** After analyzing the data sets to identify patterns and trends, data scientists will develop data models and algorithms to predict the future. They might enhance the caliber of their product offerings or data by utilizing machine learning techniques.

6.2. How Can You Get a Job as Database Administrator?

Generally, obtaining employment as a Database Administrator (DBA) necessitates a blend of learning, abilities, and networking.

The following actions can assist you in pursuing a career as a DBA:

1. **Educational Background:** A bachelor's degree in a relevant discipline, such management information systems, computer science, or information technology, is a good place to start. Even if it's not always required, having a degree can be quite beneficial, particularly for larger companies.

2. **Acquire Relevant Skills:** Learn and become proficient with database management systems (DBMS), including PostgreSQL, MySQL, Oracle, and Microsoft SQL Server. Recognize NoSQL and SQL (Structured Query Language) databases. Gain a thorough understanding of the concepts of database design, normalization, and data modeling. Learn about performance tuning, backup and recovery, and data security. Become familiar with the tools used for database administration.

3. **Certifications:** Think about earning certifications in relation to particular database management systems (DBMSs), such as Microsoft Certified Database Administrator (MCDBA), Oracle Certified Professional (OCP), or others. Possessing certifications might show prospective employers how knowledgeable you are.

4. **Obtain Real-World Experience:** To develop a portfolio, work on your own projects or make contributions to open-source database initiatives. Look for entry-level careers that require working with databases, internships, or part-time jobs. This practical experience is really beneficial.

5. **Engage in Professional Organizations and Networking:** To network with industry professionals, go to conferences, seminars, and meetings. Participate in database-related online forums and communities to network with seasoned DBAs and keep abreast of market developments.
6. **Create an Online Presence:** Make a LinkedIn profile that accentuates your abilities and background. Write blog entries or articles on databases to share your expertise.
7. **Post a Resume:** Search job boards, company websites, and your network for available positions. Make sure to emphasize your relevant experience and talents in both your cover letter and CV. A technical interview will evaluate your problem-solving abilities and database expertise, so be ready for it.
8. **Be Patient and Adaptable:** Junior DBA roles or entry-level jobs could be the first step. Get expertise to advance in the industry.
9. **Ongoing Education:** Database administration is a field that is always changing. Keep abreast of the newest developments in technology and fashion.
10. **Soft Talents:** Gain proficiency in problem-solving and communication. DBAs frequently have to collaborate with different teams and users to comprehend their data requirements and difficulties.

Keep in mind that the need for DBAs and your location can affect the job market, so be ready to move if needed. Additionally, you can differentiate yourself from other applicants by demonstrating your enthusiasm and commitment to the field through side projects and ongoing education.

6.3. How Has Cloud Computing Changed the DBA's Role?

With the introduction of cloud computing, database administrator responsibilities have changed dramatically. DBAs now have to be proficient with cloud-based platforms instead of handling hardware and software that are located on-site.

This calls for new abilities and knowledge as well as a distinct method of working. Working with many database types, including MySQL, MongoDB, and Cassandra, is a must for DBAs. Additionally, they must be knowledgeable about cloud-based resources and services like Microsoft Azure and Amazon Web Services (AWS). Through

One of the most significant changes is that DBAs are no longer responsible for managing the underlying infrastructure. With cloud computing, this is all managed by the provider. As a result, DBAs now perform more strategic tasks, such as data analytics, user experience design, and cybersecurity. DBAs often work directly with users and business leaders on developing new ways to use data and software to automate processes, reduce costs, and stay competitive.

The fact that DBAs are no longer in charge of overseeing the underlying infrastructure is among the biggest adjustments. This is entirely handled by the cloud computing provider. DBAs increasingly handle more strategic responsibilities like cybersecurity, UX design, and data analytics. DBAs frequently collaborate closely with corporate executives and users to create novel applications of data and software that streamline workflows, cut expenses, and maintain competitiveness.

DBAs need to acquire new skills for this. Strong technical abilities used to be the most crucial prerequisite. With cloud computing, these abilities are less necessary. Rather, in order to comprehend users' demands and business environment, DBAs must interact and engage with users. In order to help provide software that will answer business challenges, they must also collaborate with other teams, like DevOps.

All things considered, cloud computing is having a big impact on how a DBA performs their job. To succeed in their positions, DBAs must have the flexibility to adjust to these changes.

6.4. Automating Database Management

The level of automation in database administration determines the manpower and skills needed to manage databases. On the other hand, a system with little automation will take a large team of experts to maintain; each DBA may be responsible for 5–10 databases. As an alternative, a company may decide to automate a sizable portion of the work that may be completed by hand, therefore lowering the level of expertise needed to complete duties. The organization's workforce requirements divide as automation rises into two categories: highly skilled professionals who design and oversee the automation, and a group of less skilled "line" DBAs who carry out the automation.

Work involving database management is intricate, repetitive, time-consuming, and heavily training-required. Because databases contain important and vital information, employers typically want individuals with several years of experience. DBAs frequently have to work at off-peak hours to maintain databases (e.g., for scheduled after-hours downtime, in the case of a database-related outage or if performance has been substantially impaired). Generally speaking, DBAs receive generous pay for their lengthy hours.

Database recovery is a crucial ability that is frequently disregarded when choosing a DBA (as part of disaster recovery). When a database fails, it's not a matter of "if" but rather "when," with failures ranging from minor glitches to whole catastrophic failures. The failure could be caused by user mistake, media failure, or corrupted data. To avoid losing data in either scenario, the DBA needs to be able to restore the database to a specific point in time.

Conclusion

In the technologically advanced world of today, data reigns supreme. The function of a database administrator (DBA) has grown in importance as organizations in this digital age depend more and more on data to make decisions. A DBA is in charge of the database system's upkeep, security, and performance inside a company. Many database systems, such as Oracle, Microsoft Azure, IBM Db2, PostgreSQL, and MySQL, are covered by the DBA certifications. They offer a thorough grasp of data recovery, performance optimization, security, and database architecture.

Now you got it all.....go for it!

Table of Figures

Don't miss out!

Visit the website below and you can sign up to receive emails whenever Patrick Mukosha publishes a new book. There's no charge and no obligation.

https://books2read.com/r/B-A-HJNZ-UPBQC

BOOKS 2 READ

Connecting independent readers to independent writers.

Did you love *"Careers in Information Technology: Database Administrator"*? Then you should read *"Careers in ICT: Network and Systems Administrator"*[1] by Patrick Mukosha!

In **"Careers in ICT: *Network and Systems Administrator*"**, I offer readers an insightful and comprehensive guide to the dynamic and rapidly evolving field of network and systems administration within the realm of Information and Communication Technology (ICT). This one-page summary will provide you with a glimpse of the key themes and takeaways from the book.

Understanding the Role(s): The book begins by dissecting the roles and responsibilities of network and systems administrators, emphasizing their pivotal position in the IT industry. Readers will gain a clear understanding of the critical functions these professionals perform,

---

1. https://books2read.com/u/baq76a

2. https://books2read.com/u/baq76a

including network setup, maintenance, security, and system optimization.

Skills and Qualifications: To excel in this field, I delve into the essential skills and qualifications necessary for aspiring network and systems administrators. From technical competencies in network protocols, hardware, and software to soft skills like problem-solving, communication, and adaptability, this book guides readers in building a well-rounded skillset.

Evolving Technology: The ICT landscape is ever-evolving, and staying abreast of emerging technologies is imperative. My book explores the latest trends in network and systems administration, including cloud computing, virtualization, and cybersecurity, to help professionals remain competitive in their careers.

Certifications and Training: Certifications play a crucial role in advancing one's career. **"Careers in ICT:** *Network and Systems Administrator"*, highlights the most recognized certifications in the field, such as CompTIA Network+, Cisco CCNA, and Microsoft MCSA. I also provide guidance on choosing the right training programs and resources to prepare for these certifications.

Career Advancement: The book addresses long-term career prospects and advancement opportunities for network and systems administrators. Readers will learn about various paths, including becoming network architects, IT managers, or even transitioning into related fields like cybersecurity.

Work Challenges: Network and systems administrators face unique challenges in their day-to-day work. From dealing with network outages to handling security breaches, I offer practical advice on how to navigate these challenges effectively.

Industry Insights: The book goes beyond the technical aspects of the job and provides valuable insights into the culture and expectations of the ICT industry. Understanding the industry's dynamics, ethics, and professional networking is crucial for a successful career.

Real-World Examples: Throughout the book, I include real-world case studies and anecdotes from experienced network and systems administrators. These stories provide a glimpse into the practical aspects of the job and inspire readers to learn from the experiences of others.

"Careers in ICT: *Network and Systems Administrator"*, is a must-read for anyone considering a career in network and systems administration or looking to advance their existing career in this field. This book offers a roadmap for success, enabling individuals to make informed decisions, acquire the necessary skills, and excel in the ever-evolving world of ICT. Whether you are a recent graduate, a career changer, or an experienced IT professional, this book will be your guide to a rewarding and fulfilling career in network and systems administration.

Also by Patrick Mukosha

GoodMan
Resilient Strategies: Thriving in Harsh Business Conditions
Strategic Entrepreneurship: Navigating The Path To Success
Decisive Power: Navigating How to Make Toughest Decisions
"Reigning the Boardroom: A Trailblazing Guide to Corporate
Governance Success"
Fortifying Digital Fortress: A Comprehensive Guide to Information
Systems Security
"Unleashing the Power of Inclusive Innovation: Transforming the
World for All"
"Exploring Computer Systems: From Fundamentals to Advanced
Concepts"
"Computer Viruses Unveiled: Types, Trends and Mitigation Strategies"
"The Pinnacle of Success: Unveiling the World's 20 Most Successful
Brands in 2023"
"Mastering Relational Databases: From Fundamentals to Advanced
Concepts"
"Navigating Change: A Comprehensive Guide to Change
Management"
"Information Systems Unraveled: Exploring the Core Concepts"
"Careers in ICT: Network Engineer"
"Careers in ICT: Network and Systems Administrator"
"Careers in Information Technology: Database Administrator"

About the Author

Patrick Mukosha is a Management Consultant originally from Kitwe, Copperbelt Province of Zambia. He has a Doctorate in Management (Strategic Management) and Masters (Strategic Planning) from Atlantic International University, USA. He also holds a bachelor's in Information Technology from University of East Anglia, Norwich, UK, and a Diploma in Business Management from Canterbury College of Technology, Canterbury, UK. Member of the Institute for Leadership Development, York University, USA (2001–08), He was elected Vice President-Midlands of Computer Society of Zambia (2004), Executive Director for VISION-2011 – a consortium of NGOs (2009 – 2011, Founder of Strategic Management Community of Zambia (2017), Vice Chairperson Mungule Ward Development Committee (2021-2026). He has worked for more than 15 years for International IT and Telecommunication companies in senior management portfolios. After finishing his PhD in 2017, he embarked on career as a Management Consultant. He has worked on several Strategic Planning projects and conducts coaching and mentorship in Entrepreneurship, Business Management, Strategic Management and ICT. He's an aggressive serial entrepreneur and founder of PatWest Technologies.